MEET ME IN THE MEADOW

A Collection of Poems, Short Stories and Memoirs

Andrea Downing Doetzel

AuthorHouse™ LLC
1663 Liberty Drive
Bloomington, IN 47403
www.authorhouse.com
Phone: 1-800-839-8640

Published by AuthorHouse 11/27/2013

ISBN: 978-1-4918-1581-6 (sc)
     978-1-4918-1582-3 (e)

Library of Congress Control Number: 2013916373

authorHOUSE®

Introduction

Andrea wrote her first poem about Spring in 3th grade. Two teachers praised her for the best in the class and her uncle Charles Guenther, an internationally known poet, translator and literary reviewer for the St. Louis Post Dispatch, noticed her interest in writing. All through her creative years he gave his encouragement and became her mentor. Years went by with no further writing until her adult years after her children finally left home. She started writing a Christmas Poem to put in with cards during the holidays. Friends wrote her back on cards she would receive the next year, asking for another poem to share with their families over the new holiday season. This became a new challenge and tradition.

Eventually she wrote other poems that were published in local newspapers and magazines. She became a member of St. Louis Poetry Center founded by her uncle Charles and as her collection grew she was featured in an article in the Jefferson County Journal. Several other poems were published in the Cahokian Magazine. The Shoppers Review newspaper in Highland, Illinois featured several in a column written by Burnell Petry a/k/a The Sugar Creek Wanderer, and he introduced her to the Highland League of Writers Group where she became a member and started writing short stories.

A variety from her collection is now her first book, **Meet Me in the Meadow**.

Andrea at age 7   -   Photo by her Uncle Charles Guenther, poet and Translator.

They share the same Birthday - April 29th

Andrea <u>Downing </u>Doetzel was born in south St. Louis and grew up with a love of nature and the outdoors and sometimes her own fantasy world, to the dismay of grade school teachers who always noticed her daydreaming in class. She yearned to be outside frolicking in the sunshine and grew up near two city parks where she spent many hours with her brother and sister. She loved to pick flowers and jump in huge piles of leaves in the fall.

Now older with two grown children and a grandson she has found more time to write after retirement from her career as an Insurance Service Representative. After losing her husband of 45 years, she moved on and currently resides on a friend's farm in Illinois enjoying many more adventures than the city parks she frequented in her youth. She loves organic greenhouse gardening and is learning new things about plants, birds and wildlife around the area.

She has a background in dance, starting at an early age when her mother taught Tap, Ballet and Toe and she went on to continue in many different forms as an adult. A member of Simone's Seventh Veil Dance company for many years she performed in local St. Louis Greek and ethnic restaurants and later went on to compete in Roller Skate Dancing placing first in her region and continuing to the national level with her dance partner David. Later she and her sister Claudia, joined an Ice Dance Ensemble and competed locally for 5 years. An interest in archaeology for more than 20 years is reflected in several of her poems in her "I dig archaeology" section.

After living in Arnold for 33 years, a City buyout forced a move to a new location and the most likely place to build was on a 23 acre tract of land she and her husband and son co-owned in Barnhart. Virgin woods on most of the grounds became her own new state park, complete with springs and a bluff overlooking Glaize Creek. The dense woods beyond had a path leading to a lowland she calls the "meadow". (The name chosen for the title of this book.) She enjoyed many adventures here, with her family. Her son now owns and lives on the land and she visits it often going back to her special place where she sits in the meadow to read or write. Way back in the woods Andrea discovered a secret "Place" on one of her walks with the family dog and has included a 3 part narrative that describe this experience as she and her canine friend venture back again and again.

Meet me in the Meadow

Would you like to hear my stories?

Some are Fantasy, Some true

Then meet me in the Meadow

And I will tell my tales to you...

Table of Contents

Family

Just for Fun

I "DIG" Archaeology

Stories

FAMILY

SOUL SEARCHING

In a quiet cemetery
On a lonely country road
Rests a group of my ancestors
That endured the days of old

They settled near the Fabius
Purchased tracts of timber land
To clear for farms and homesteads
With sons and neighbors to lend a hand

The frontier life was difficult
Sometimes heartbreak took its toll
When they had to lay a child to rest
Hoping Heaven would find its soul

Many more children were buried here
As years passed, the settlers too
Anderson's married into other clans
And the number of headstones grew

Downing, Greenley, Hendren
Are the names upon these graves
At one end a row of unmarked stones
Where they buried loyal slaves

In the center a tall Cedar grows
Deeply rooted in the ground
Branching out like the tree of my family
Lying still and silent now

If they could speak and tell me
Of the past, their tales untold
I might compare them with who I am
As I watch my life unfold.

TRUE GRIT AND MUSH

They say our ancestors were tough ones, had True Grit and lived through strife. That the younger generations are as soft as Mush and live a very pampered life.

How did they handle a typical day? Well, let us just compare. From a simple task like fixing breakfast, to the time they combed their hair!

The rooster crows at Five A.M. and gets me up and out the door into the rain to bring in wood for the stove. Stack it on the floor and then get the fire started. Back outside and over to the smokehouse to carve a slab of bacon and over to the chicken coop to gather a dozen eggs. Don't forget to milk the cow on the way and get some coffee beans to grind from the storeroom. Add wood to the fire and grind coffee beans, mix up biscuit dough, cut up bacon and fix with eggs.

Breakfast served at 10:00 A.M.. Clean up the dishes later or you will not be finished in time to start feeding the chickens. Gather laundry for a trip with the washboard to the creek to scrub and then hang the heavy overalls on the line. Be sure to remember to put on a pot to boil for starch while you are mending a few pair of ripped pants. Ooops, we are almost out of candles, so need to pour some melted tallow in the molds so we can have light to read by tonight.

Then the greens need to be soaked and pies baked for supper before you can start thinking about what to have for lunch. It is time to bake bread again as we are getting low and the dogs are still barking for their morning meal and it is1:00 P.M. Peel the apples for the pies and feed the dogs the apple peelings with leftover bacon grease to keep them happy for a while until you get a chance to clean up the breakfast dishes so they can have the scraps.

Oh my, I just passed the mirror in the bedroom and saw that I have not even combed my hair yet today. Make the beds and get out the long underwear to mend while the pies are baking. If hubby comes home from town where he went to sell a hog, I guess I can toss him some apple peelings to keep him pacified until I can fix his lunch. Oh, what was that? Sounds like the baby is crying again. I guess I forgot to warm its bottle this morning and feed it after I milked the cow!

Come to think of it, as I recall the pail full of milk is still out in the barn as I had my hands full of bacon and eggs. Oh well, by this time I am ready to feed him some oatmeal for lunch. The hogs need to be fed now so I will comb my hair later as it is still raining outside. The overalls are getting wet on the line so now I have to lug them in and hang these dripping things from the rafters to dry. Stoke up the stove again.

By now I need more firewood and it is still wet when I bring it in. I am really disgusted as the pies burned while I was out getting more wood and checking on the hogs and so I toss the apple peelings and the burned pies out the window to the hogs and the dogs and hope this will count for their supper. Mending by hand takes a long time and it is now 5:00 P.M..

Hubby still is not home yet so I just fix a pot of beans with bacon and mix up some cornbread. He probably stopped at the neighbor's farm on the way home to check that crooked wheel that is always falling off of the wagon.

The cows need to be called in now as it is getting dark and coyotes are around. I need to feed the baby again. Thank goodness it stopped raining. I just remembered, I forgot to eat my own lunch today and still have not cleaned up the breakfast dishes.

Hubby arrives back home at 9:00 P.M. as he stopped at the neighbors for supper. He smelled burned pies on the way home and made a U turn over to the next farm. His clothes were all gritty when he came in as the wagon wheel broke and tossed him in a mud puddle. His clothes will need to be soaked but he will need to take a bath in the washtub first. But the firewood is low again from all the cooking and it is too dark to go down to the creek for more water. Anyway the washtub is still down at the creek full of dirty diapers that I forgot to wash this morning. Have to do them tomorrow as I am running behind. It is now 10:00 P.M.. I am really tired so I guess I won't read much tonight and I am not going to bother to comb my hair before turning in and hubby will have to take his bath in the creek tomorrow, I sure hope it doesn't rain anymore tonight as I would sure like the wood to dry out so I can heat up the stove to boil water for tomorrow. Sigh.............. What a day!

The automatic alarm on Mr. Coffeemaker wakes me up at 7:00 A.M. with the smell of a freshly brewed pot. I get up, put on my robe and open the Coffemate jar. I find the Sizzlean in the refrig to nuke in the microwave, put the pop tarts in the toaster while opening a can of frozen orange juice. Then scramble some eggs and clean up the pan. Breakfast served at 7:30 A.M. Get the kids out the front door with lunch money and snacks to wait by the mailbox for the school bus. Let the dog out back and then I head back inside for a leisurely bubble bath. Then blow dry my hair and dress and flip the remote to catch the 8:00 A.M. morning news update before heading out to the mall to shop till I drop. I am sure to pack a granola bar for my mid-morning snack after my 10:00 A.M. exercise class. Stop by the cleaners on my way home from the library and pick up McDonald's for lunch. Do three loads of laundry in the washer and dryer and hang up the permanent press in all the closets. Then it is time for the 2:00 Soap Operas that continue till 4:30. Pick up the kids from ball practice and head home with rented movies from the video store and the free Pizza you get with the movies as it is too hot to cook tonight. 7:00 P.M. and after homework and supper, I put in the video movie and can hardly pick up the remote as I am soooo tired. Whew................. What a day!

That night Modern Miss was awakened in her bed

There was a haggard old spirit floating overhead

That said:

BOO HOO HOO – POOR LITTLE YOU!

My Great Grandfather - Willis Anderson   My Great Grandmother - Hettie Anderson

THE ICE CREAM MAN WITH RHYTHM

The Ice Cream Man with Rhythm
Came cruising down my street one day
The clanging of his clear brass bell
Could be heard three blocks away

Clang, Clang, Clang Clang   (slow)
Ding, Ding, Ding, Ding, Ding (fast)
So catchy was that rhythm
The way his bell would ring

He was probably out of high school
And a part time ice cream man
Then moonlighted as a drummer
Of a local hard rock band

Other drivers seemed monotonous
No creative sense of tune
I would tire of hearing them
By the first weekend in June

I used to dread these peddlers
Selling tinted flavored ice
In the flimsy paper wrappers
For their inflated price

Always on the traveled route
To arrive at supper time
I'd grit my teeth, resent these creeps
Who made my children whine

I guess that I have mellowed
As the years have passed
My children grown and married
Kids of their own at last

Now I'm "toe tappin" curbside
With change purse in my hand
Next to my toddler grandchild
Who awaits the ice cream man

When my grandmother, at age 3 months, was kidnapped by an old Gypsy woman behind their home on Osceola and Broadway around the time of the St. Louis World'sFair, and recovered by the neighbor, the story was told over and over to family and children and grandchildren of the next generations. I was particularly interested in hearing it directly from my grandmother herself as she described how her older siblings told her how they all ran screaming after the caravan with the neighbor man in his wagon following behind to help the family with the rescue as my great grandfather was still at work in St. Louis. I used to try to imagine why an old gypsy woman would want to kidnap a small baby girl and my thoughts led me to write the "Old Traveler" and Marietta".

My grandmother, Hulda C. Schuessler at age 16

Who was the: "small girl child recovered" from the gypsy caravan at age 3 months.

Mother of Hilda Anne Guenther and Charles Guenther, famous poet and translator.

When my grandmother was a small baby, the family lived in a small house on Osceola and Broadway in South St. Louis. There was a vast meadow in back of the row of small houses in this neighborhood. A creek next to a trail beyond the grassy area was a thoroughfare for Gypsy Caravans as they rolled by in the evenings. They were heading west after work in the city.

The St. Louis World's Fair was planned for 1904. Many manual laborers were needed and were hired from these traveling gypsy bands in the years before the Fair. My Great Grandmother had warned her older children not to leave anything outside the house after they finished their chores because it may vanish, taken by gypsies overnight.

One pleasant fall day my Great Grandmother placed her youngest child, a 3 month old baby girl (my grandma) in her bassinet on the screened back porch to finish her nap while she went back in the kitchen to prepare supper. The older children played in front and things were quiet in the back of the house, until Grandma heard a tapping at the back door. She greeted an old gypsy woman who had gone down the back of the row of houses begging for handouts and looking for work. Great Grandma had no work, but offered to share some things and went back inside to see what she could find. Back on the porch the baby was missing and she screamed. The children playing in front ran after the woman who was making her way far across the field with the baby in her arms. One of the older children got the neighbor to help in the chase with his horse and wagon. The children all jumped in the back and took off yelling as they closed in on this band of thieves.

My grandmother was taken back home safely and the Caravan slowly rode off toward the sunset with no further incident. I was always intrigued by this story as I tried to imagine why an old woman would want to steal an infant. The last few verses of "An Old Traveler" are what I thought the reason could be. Maybe a plan to train the girl to dance for trinkets as a source of income for the tribe, as it was a tradition passed down through generations of European Gypsy bands.   Whatever wishes she had for my grandmother were not followed through. But the future generations of daughters and granddaughters were intrigued by the world of dance and all started at a young age and continued performing and teaching dance in many forms throughout their lives.

The poem "Marietta" is what I imagined my grandmother would have grown up to be like if the Gypsy woman would have escaped and traveled far out of reach of the family that day. My grandmother grew up a very beautiful woman with brown eyes and dark flowing hair. She could have passed for a Gypsy if she would have been raised in their world.   My mother, also with dark hair, was an Adagio dancer at age 15 and performed on the stage of the Fox Theatre on Grand Avenue in St. Louis. . She taught Tap and Ballet at the Lion's Den in Kirkwood Missouri on Saturday mornings for many years beginning at age 15. Later she attended William Woods College where she instructed students in dance, acrobatics, marching drill teams, gym classes and team sports. My mother continued teaching dance in many forms into middle age. My sister and I also grew up dancing and I branched off into Middle Eastern Dance and later, Roller Skate Ballroom dancing and was a member of an Ice Dance Ensemble. My daughter and two nieces, now grown, were also active in dance, performing at young ages.

AN OLD TRAVELER

They came from many countries
To journey to this land
Across the great Atlantic
to travel west in bands

Their wagons rolled across the plains
They trailed the creeks and streams
Camping for a night or two
then following their dreams

A crafty breed they proved to be
Making do with what they had
But pilfering their other needs
by sending out a young lad

Approaching a large city
beyond the river wide
In hopes of finding work for some
once on the other side

A World's Fair was coming
In the many months ahead
The work these hearty men could do
would keep this large group fed

They settled near the Fairgrounds
but grew restless with the pace
Moving further out each week
In search of open space

In back of my Great Grandma's house
their wagons came one day
A beggar woman at the door
requesting work for pay

Her keen eyes surveyed the cottage
with the sun porch in the rear
An infant there lie sleeping
In the cool afternoon air

There was no work at our place
to help with on that day
But Great Grandma went to find her purse
to help the woman on her way

A search for a few coins
and old clothing and some food
back to the porch to greet the guest
but she had vanished where she stood

Across the field she hurried
Toward her moving caravan
A bundle stashed beneath her shawl
within reach they lent a hand

Our neighbors heard the screaming
when they discovered the babe gone
and ran after moving wagons
traveling toward the setting sun

The small girl child recovered
the aging woman sad
Many sons were born to her
Daughters she never had

She had been a famous dancer
of the people of her kind
in search of one to carry on
the traditional art in mind

The neighbors left the wagon
with the small child safe in arms
they checked her over quickly
and she had not been harmed

They looked back toward the old one
She pointed with raised arms
and uttered some strange foreign phrase
as if to scold and warn

My mother became a teacher of dance
accomplished as a young girl
she loved the earthy ethnic style
with leaps and spins and twirls

And I learned Middle Eastern dance
and taught this style as well
Were the daughters of the small one
cast under a gypsy spell?

Hilda Anne Guenther

Age 16

Saturday Dance Classes

Lion's Den Lodge

Kirkwood, MO

Teacher - Hilda Anne Guenther

Bottom Left

Hilda Anne Guenther

My mother at age 17

Andrea Downing Doetzel

At age 41 - in

Middle Eastern Dance

Performing with

Simone's Seventh Veil Dance Co.

MARIETTA

Beneath an autumn starlit sky
As campfire flames burn bright
The visitors arrive by group
Anticipating the night

The violins begin to play
A festive mood spreads round
With room left near the crackling fire
They listen for the sound…

She leaps down from her wagon
With a rattling tambourine
Bare legs flash as she twirls in
To captivate the scene

From over a bare shoulder
She casts a dark eyed glance
And is caught up in the spirit
Of her swirling gypsy dance

The glint of golden earrings
Beneath flowing raven hair
A bangled hand holds ruffled skirt
She seems to tempt and dare

A slower tempo, her body sways
Moving slender graceful arms
She smiles and gives that knowing look
To those captured by her charms

A turn now for her final spin
Her sultry dance complete
As a thousand coins and trinkets
Are tossed at dusty suntanned feet

Andrea Doetzel 11-1990

WHAT DID THE BALD
MAN SAY WHEN HE GOT
A COMB FOR CHRISTMAS?

"I'LL NEVER PART WITH IT."
— A. — THANKS!

UNCLE D. AND ME

He sends me cute cartoons and things
And I send him my rhymes
I'm proud he calls me "favorite niece"
We've shared some special times

He is my inspiration
my mentor, pal and friend
Time flies when we're together
but too soon visits end

A unique personality
with great humor, charm and wit
His jokes and funny stories
sometimes give me laughing fits.

I remember him from early years
his kind ways, sincere and true
our friendship grew quite special
He seems to calm me when I'm blue

We both like the family history
have wondered how we compare
He wrote all about our ancestors
and wonderful books he shared

Somehow personalities clicked
similar genes, I'd say
or maybe kindred spirits
from a past life still at play

I can't wait for our next meeting
my heartstrings feel a tug
I must see what he's been up to
and get another great big hug!!!

Love, Andrea

COO!
COO!

UNCLE D AND ME

He sends me cute cartoons and things
And I send him my rhymes
I'm proud he calls me "favorite niece"
We've shared some special times

He is my inspiration
My mentor, pal and friend
Time flys when we're together
But too soon visits end

A unique personality
With great humor, charm and wit
His jokes and funny stories
Sometimes give me laughing fits

I remember him from early years
His kind ways, sincere and true
Our friendship grew quite special
He seems to calm me when I'm blue

We both love the family history
Have wondered how we compare
He wrote all about our ancestors
And wonderful books he shared

Somehow personalities clicked
Similar genes I'd say
Or maybe kindred spirits
From a past life still at play

I can't wait till our next meeting
My heartstrings feel a tug
I must see what he's been up to
And get another great big hug!

Just For Fun

LADY BUGS THAT BUG YOU

Don't fear a little ladybug if it lands upon your nose

It just wants to give a hug while resting tiny toes

And it sure likes freckles, must be drawn to you by spots

So if you want more visits, start wearing polka dots

If it gets tangled in your hair just lightly give a tug

Or simply shoo it on it's way toward the nearest shrub

It's favorite thing, to soar around and keep itself in flight

Exploring bright warm summer days before the dark of night

It's not a creepy crawler like a waterbug or a mite

Or a gigantic poison spider that could give you such a fright

It's not slithery and slimy like a nightcrawler or slug

And certainly not big like that hard shelled brown June bug

No likeness to a grasshopper or any kind of cricket

That can jump up to scare you as it springs out of a thicket

Crickets roam and sing at night while hidden near the ground

Grasshoppers spit that ugly stuff, like a tobacco brown

If it was like a lunar moth or a fragile butterfly

It would be hard to catch them, but you could try and try

So of all the insect creatures, I hope that you will see

Those gentle harmless lady bugs want love, like you and me

WOOLY CURIOUS WORM

Here you show yourself again this cool September Day

  Resting on a Maple leaf as the cool breeze makes it sway.

You show your stripes of brown or rust upon your darker back

  Each year you have a different look, sometimes you're mostly black.

They say your coat can tell us how the winter soon will be

  But since I am a skeptic, please satisfy my curiosity

How do I remember what the width of your stripes mean?

  Thin or wide or none at all, or somewhere in between

Will winter days be cold or mild, will we have tons of snow?

  These things you know are vital, to a person on the go.

There has got to be a catch phrase that will help us all remember

  What your different stripes will mean when you show up in September

THE PURPLE ESCAPE

Gosh, Thanksgiving and Christmas will be here very soon
Got to get the house all ready, and clean out every room

The fridge has all these leftovers, just hanging around
Some outdated veggies and Oh, look what I found…..

A whole bowl of Concord Grapes we picked in September
What is this up in the freezer? Some Blueberries, I remember

The holidays are always full of things I have created
I think I'll make some beverage with this fruit that is outdated

Get out the metal strainer and a mixing bowl
Crush fruit, remove the seeds, get a good pulp I am told

Add some sugar and a little water, mix it up real fine
No time to ferment this stuff, so add some REAL wine

Have half a bottle of Cabernet and some sweet Merlot
To compare the real taste test, more sampling as you go

Add more wine and club soda to make this beverage bubble
Sample more and hold it up to see a glass of "Purple Trouble"

Must be losing track of time as the clock is looking weird
I don't think my cleaning will get done now, as I feared

Another sample, a big glass now and I have never felt like this
I have a secret recipe that I will call "My Purple Bliss"

Buzzzzzz…………………   Zzzzzzzz……………………

By Andrea Doetzel   11-13-11

RAINY DAY DUMPS

Here I sit and watch the rain, as it splatters on the windowpane

Can't go out again this morning, now a new rain and hail warning

Root bound plants wait in peat pots, to find a space in garden plots

Each day I watch the weather charts, to see when clear so planting starts

Soggy mud gets my boots stuck, can't run the mower with any luck

Easter Flowers have come and gone, Rain day and night and again till dawn

Who can reap or sow or mow, All rain does is make weeds grow!

THE DUMB BLOND METEOROLOGIST

Did you ever think of using a simple lost bird feather
To predict your local atmospheric changes in the weather?

I moved to the country where soft prairie breezes blow
And sometimes stronger straight line winds the weather man won't show

I'm tired of watching TV and hear radio stations bark
This NOAA thing is great for some, but I don't need an ark.

Media gives the detailed stuff of counties all around
Some of the storms are miles away, can't do me any harm

So I'll just go on through my day predicting <u>my own</u> weather
Nailed to my front porch way up high? A brand new turkey feather

This concept is not new you see, as Ozark people tell
With no TV or radio it has proved to serve them well.

Simply check the feather daily for changes you may see
Like if it's wet or dry, to confirm predictability

If it is shivering in the breeze, it means it's very cold
If it's soaked and soggy, it means hard rain I am told

If it should freeze when soaking wet, this means ice and snow
So you can plan your day accordingly of where you have to go

But if you find the feather gone, start heading for the barn
Take cover for tornado winds CAN do you lots of harm

Hold tight to a fixed object as these strong southwest winds blast
And hope the barn don't fall in, and collapse down on your _ _ _!

LOOSY GOOSE LUCY

My sister Claudia lives in a subdivision in Fenton, Missouri near south St. Louis County.

The common grounds of the neighborhood have a small lake with a center fountain

where Canadian geese and Mallard ducks inhabit the nearby grassland areas. Each

Spring the mating geese look for new nesting grounds. It is not unusual to find a nest of

Geese or duck eggs under a porch or shrub lined areas of the homes there. One Spring

My sister discovered a nest of over 8 huge eggs under a bush near her front doorsteps.

Year after year the suspected same goose chose her yard to settle in, forcing her to

Become a broom swishing gal to chase the population away and take back her homestead.

This poem was written for my sister, Claudia and her Canadian geese challenges.

LOOSY GOOSE LUCY

Lucy Goosy was quite a tart

She was out to steal a few hearts

Strutting round, and quite able

Legs like Betty Grable

All set to outwit and outsmart

She was single, and not yet life mated

And monogamy she truly hated

Why not have lots of fun

When you are still young

Cause life with one male? - overrated

With no other gals to be found

All sitting on nests at home grounds

She heard males honk and growl

As she pranced they would howl

And she flipped her tail feathers around

The first one to score, Alexander

A studly young long feathered gander

But he lost interest soon

When he saw a full moon

Thinking he would be cursed and then slandered

Lucy then tried a new guy each night

Soon her belly grew way out of sight

She laid eggs by the ton

Different colors, each one

A huge nest built in her state of fright

She was stuck in a motherly way

No more time for nightlife and play

Hatchin eggs was not fun

Carefree days were now done

A lesson learned, you play, you pay

Her new goslings then strutted around

Other mothers made loud hissing sounds

Each of her chicks had her looks

Her bad genes somehow took

Twelve new tail flipping floozies in town

A parade led by shamed Lucy Goosy, as her chicks wiggled to the Watusi, Now this can't be too good.

So they say as they should….. There goes the whole neighborhood!

CORNCOBS

Old Corncobs are not for snobs

They are for the very bold

Mostly used by country folks

Who lived in days of old

At the corner of the outhouse

In the pail, a grand supply

Red or white, just choose one

Watch out for field mice on the sly

Someone used up the Catalog

That sat upon the shelf

They tore out the fashion pages

I was saving for myself

Oh well, when they visit next

I'll have cast my magic spell

A lurking spider beneath the seat

Will bite and make them yell

Sitting around with a group of friends about the same age and reflecting back on the

Good old days, some of them remembered their childhood experience of living in rural

areas or on farms where plumbing was a luxury.   Once you are used to city life and indoor

plumbing it is so strange to be expected to use a primitive outhouse. I remember the surprise

of visiting my grandma's old farm in Northern Missouri and spending a summer vacation

weekend there. I had to discover the way to the toilette" as I eventually called it.

Our group discussed the different things in these structures, such as, two seaters, a bucket

of lime, catalog or magazines, various flies, moths, spiders and their webs in the corners,

and finally at the older farms, the familiar bucket of corncobs resting in the corner. We then

laughed and giggled and thanked the Lord for modern times and indoor plumbing.   Amen

ERIN GOES BRALESS

Erin went braless, and her body's not flawless

    From Step Dancing at such a young age

A child thin as a twig, in her red curly wig

    She bounced a lot doing her jig

As she started to grow, the dance took its toll

    And soon sagging started to show

All her friends in their teens, wore supports of dark green

    To keep themselves safe from that scene

As days went by, these young gals caught the eye

    and young lads snuck a glance on the sly

Megan, Patsy and Shannon got lots of attention

    Guys saw perky parts that I will not mention

Erin had damage done, Dancin no longer fun

    In a downhill decline with no stoppin

And she couldn't be free of the pain in her knee

    While her chest upper parts were a floppin

No more dancin she chose, a retired Irish Rose

    With a hunched over posture and pose

Soon she needed a cane, from short walks she'd refrain

Later housebound and crippled in pain

So a lesson learned here, take care how you appear

You must practice to become a good "Do Bee"

Hold em up and beware, of your precious young pair

Cause it's hard to replace saggy boobies!

RHYME AND ME

Although it might be out of fashion, Rhyme and Meter is my passion

      Some say this style is well outworn

      Why limit yourself to a closed form

      Write some prose and you will see

      Creative expression is born free

But as I write thoughts and feelings down, they end up with a rhyming sound

      Fond childhood memories I recall

      The glowing nightlight in the hall

      Bedside Mom or Gramps would smile

      And tell tall tales or joke a while

      "Before I go turn out the light

      I want to wish you nighty night"

      "Close your eyes and slumber tight

      And don't let the bed bugs bite"

At school we heard it every day, the rhymes and songs in work and play

      30 days hath September

      April June and November

      I before E, except after C

      Does anyone remember these?

In High School there was Rock and Roll, time out to do the hop and stroll

The games were fun and we would scream

The cheers to help support our team

Here here, where where?

We want a touchdown over there

Then back to culture for a bit

Reciting poems in English lit

I think that I shall never see

A poem as lovely as a tree

Now how do I escape this style that dominates my brain?

The ghostly verses of the past now seem to take the blame

I think I might try writing class

To clear my mind up from the past

My goal is to learn free verse style,

De-Programming may take a while

OVAL PICTURE FRAME

Picture frame, Picture frame, I need an oval picture frame

to decorate my humble wall of family portraits, one and all

At the top the antique oval frame, where great grandma takes her reign

Next are young grandpa and ma, engaged but secret from them all

Then Mom's picture in her youth, my smiling son who lost a tooth

Daughter's wedding picture in Waterford glass, a keepsake poem from the past.

All these frames are oval shape, to deviate would not be great

I want to keep the oval theme as I make a unique stair step scene

Now, I had a milestone portrait done, when I turned 60 just for fun

So endless trips to antique malls, flea markets and old attic walls

I need a large size oval frame, for my own space that still remains

But I keep shopping in my search,   a frame to grace my oval perch

Oh Boy, look what I just found, searching the barn shelves all around.

A recycled frame to fit my face, what the heck, it'll take its place

FANTASY FAIR FOOD

This summer has been so dry and hot
    I escape my wilted garden plot

A Cooler evening with a breeze
    To a County Fair among shade trees

Oh the sights and sounds and smells
    How produce wagon contents swell

Fresh corn, tomatoes, squash and beans
    Herbs and roots, things in between

Away from the noisy carnival lot
    Where kids ride and scream a lot

Fragrance draws me to the food
    All kinds to please your every mood

Fried pickles, tomatoes, onions and such
    Then stranger things I know not much

Ever hear of a fried Twinkie?
    This treat is soggy and quite dinky

Oreo's, artichokes, fried Kool Aid?
    I saw how these FRIED things are made

I'll stick to my favorite ones
    Country fries, pulled pork on buns

Then fried green tomatoes and pickles for me
    Cotton candy, ice cream and Tums of three

By Andrea Doetzel   8-27-2011

REINDEER REBELLION

By Andrea Doetzel - orig 1994

2004 was the year Santa's
Reindeer rebelled
All stormed into Elk's lodge
While they shouted and yelled

A long deer hunting season
Left one of them shot
Donder hobbled on crutches
And still hurt a lot

They all feared for their future
One said "Life is too short"
"to keep pulling a sleigh
With a fat bearded old fart"

The trip was too long
And stretched into the night
With the last toys delivered
In the soft morning light

This year, they had ideas
Of what they'd rather do
They exchanged plans one by one
And said "Let's follow through!"

The vote was unanimous
They would stage a big strike
"It would do Santa good
To pull his sleigh with a bike"

So, Dasher signed up
for the next harness race
and went off to the horse track
in hopes of first place

Dancer got 4 tickets
To the big Christmas ball
And Prancer got them dates
With cute does from their stall

Vixen was up to
Some practical jokes
He'd fix Santa by loosening
The bicycle spokes

Comet yearned for adventure
And travel in space
To fly high among stars
With the wind in his face

Cupid tried out
As a singer of blues
And got top billing
On the next Love Boat Cruise

Poor Donder, being injured
just tried to hang loose
but got stuck in the kitchen
to cook Christmas goose

Blitzen fell off the wagon
and got totally crocked
Slept it off on the porch
cause the front door was locked

Rudolf found an old girlfriend
and asked for a date
They went off to that Ice
Rink in New York to skate

When the Six O'Clock News
heard of Santa's big plight
They sent him their News Copter
for his Christmas Eve flight

Santa jumped in the craft
gave the News team a whistle
flew away in a flash
like a fast rocket missile

All the toys were delivered
Everything was cool
Santa slept late and chuckled
as he was no fool

He called a big Reindeer meeting
at the lodge New Year's day
and as they sauntered in
some were still munching hay

Santa had some choice comments
about their last minute "Strike"
and he would deal later with
whoever messed with his bike

THEN HE SAID:

"This year's trip was a SNAP
I was NOT even tired
So, I will make it Official
You are ALL FIRED !"

" I LOVE my new aircraft
with bright lights and blades chopping
Sure beats cracking the whip
and dodging fresh reindeer droppings!"

I "DIG" Archaeology

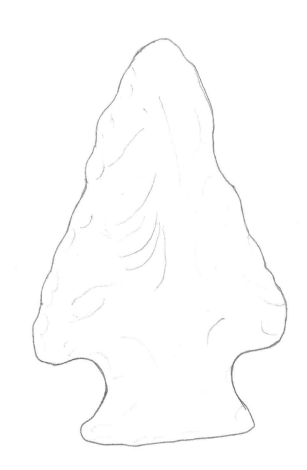

MOSS COVERED ROCKS

Beside a narrow trail they lie
On a bluff top facing west
I can overlook the stream below
And often pause here to rest

This tranquil spot will draw me
At times I wonder why
I am tempted into daydreams
While gazing at the sky

There is a special feeling here
Of stories left untold
Sensing mystery and secrets
My interest seems to grow

While sitting here I contemplate
How long this moss has grown
About the surface of the rock
If it is smooth or worn

As I peel back a ragged patch
Where the edge is dead and dry
I brush away the dust beneath
And strange shapes catch my eye

Signs and symbols carved on stone
By those from another time
To tell a tale of history
Or perhaps daydreams like mine

TOOLS OF TIME

This large flat stone atop the hill
Is where I sit and ponder
about the past and long ago
when ancient people wandered

The layers of the earth
beneath my feet reveal
the culture of these people
as if to make them real

Broken points convey the skill
of weapons they possessed
Survival was in hunting
and they would strive to make the best

Moving further back in time
the tools I find are crude
A broken celt or hand axe
with smooth edges showing use

The remnants of a fire pit
with bone and seed and shell
To hunt and gather what they could
at times they were fed well

The flesh of a great beast
would feed a tribe or two
as they followed great herds around
to stalk the chosen few

The butchering was done by all
as cuts of meat were wrapped
sinew, bone and skin all saved
back home with heavy packs

Around a campfire late at night
hunters re-lived the kill
women stitched the softened hides
tired children nearby lie still

If they took the time to daydream
while creating a new craft
was there a moment to reflect
experiences of the past?

Did they wonder about that someone
who hunted in this place
finding tools of those before them
that belonged to an earlier race?

As I hold these tools I marvel
About history and man
I feel a certain kinship
And closeness with this clan

THE WEEKEND ARCHAEOLOGIST

Tired, bored

Caked with mud

This day turned out to be a dud

Humid, hot

Covered with dust

Discovery makes work a must

Sore knees

Fighting sweat bees

Could I just find something please?

Nothing ventured

Nothing gained

I guess today it could have rained

Weary shoulders

Aching feet

A find would make my day complete

Need help

to sift through dirt and sand

for soon this will be condo land

Last week here

and at a lag

Nothing for my collection bag

Pack the car

with picks and trowels

empty buckets and damp sweat towels

One last look

at this old place

former home of an earlier race

Kick some dirt clumps

on the way back

Flint chips scatter from a crack

Must look closer

then I find

the discovery I had in mind

The perfect point

in skill and style

makes these summer days worthwhile

Andrea Doetzel   9-90

A summer of weekends. My results, in a search of an area to be developed. My wish was for some kind of artifact to remember the people who inhabited these grounds hundreds of years ago.

JESSE JAMES REMAINS UNCOVERED

Now a look back in 2012 after the event of 1995 that took place in Kearney Mo.

Living near St. Louis and traveling to the small towns in Northern Missouri where my grandparents settled on acreage from the Louisiana Purchase, I knew the area of Kearney while driving through on my way back from Colorado vacations. Many times I drove east across the upper part of Missouri to the family farm in Knox County before heading home. When I heard the news back in the summer of 1995, I was alarmed at the stories of plans to exhume the body of Jesse James. There were not too many forensic television shows on at that time and I thought it odd, not understanding a reason but then DNA testing recently became available.

Looking back now, perhaps some family inheritance or property rights were being challenged at that time for this to take place. There had been rumors that he faked his own death to escape prison from his past outlaw way of life and his descendants wanted to know if he was really buried at the gravesite bearing his name. The mystery had people intrigued as the news crews traveled to the town of Kearney and the area became saturated when merchants set up tents and sold toy guns, bandanas, souvenirs and trinkets, luring in the crowds who traveled there for the excitement that week. I was just surprised that it became such a carnival type atmosphere as people swarmed to the area in droves like in the Gold Rush days of the Old Wild West.

After the remains were exhumed and analyzed they discovered a round lead ball from a colt revolver in the area of his chest lying in the casket. He had been shot in his right lung by one of the Union Army soldiers in 1865 when he was trying to surrender near Lexington, MO and the bullet remained in his body, and was discovered in 1995. Stories from his past were told that it took two years for Jesse to heal from some sort of bullet wound. It was not the shot that killed Jesse James.

Maybe Jesse did not seek medical treatment after he was shot in the chest because his whereabouts would have been known and he just wanted to live a peaceful life with his family. The search for answers from DNA confirmed for his descendants that he was really buried in Kearney and that put an end to most of the rumors that he escaped to Texas.

You were shot while trying to surrender. You suffered with this bullet wound for 2 years. Later while trying to live a clean quiet life, another bullet ended it.

Rest in Peace Jesse James.

DIGGING UP JESSE

title revised 8-18-2012

Did they have to dig up Jesse James?

Why not just let him be?

Was there a special point to prove

Or morbid curiosity?

They swarmed the town of Kearney

Newscasters and their crew

With a special group of scientists

And the tourist crowds they drew

They dug deep down into the ground

To solve a mystery

And searched to find enough of him

To prove identity

Recovered silver casket handles

Small bits of bone and tooth

After test results on DNA

They hoped to learn the truth

But he was a human being

As well as outlaw from the West

Shouldn't Jesse lie in peace

Where he was laid to rest?

Is there anything left of Jesse?

I see his shadow drifting by

Across a silver moon, to reach

Ghost Riders in the sky

Submitted to Eric James of "Stray Leaves" and archived in The James Family Website on 8-18-2012

HOBO

On a deeply wooded hillside

Tall trees bend and sway

An old oak bears an odd name

That I found today

Perhaps a stranger passing

Made this mark upon the tree

Or a young boy carved his nickname

In the bark for all to see

Time has healed the edges

Of the letters carved down low

The spaces too have widened

As the tree went on to grow

I think now as I stand here

This "Hobo" just might be

The name of a beloved pet

Who rests beneath this tree

On a vacation trip in 1988 my husband and I visited Nashville for the first time. The days before, traveling across Oklahoma and Arkansas had been rainy and the first clear day we arrived in downtown Nashville at 3:00 in the afternoon. At last, the first sunny dry day to cut grass in the Midwest was what we thought as we saw maintenance men mowing around the public buildings in the square. But we were shocked as we noticed sleeping bodies on the lawns as the mowers buzzed around, as if the men weren't even there. One man was sleeping on his side clutching a battered old guitar. We wondered how these old men could sleep through the noise and why the lawn care staff would put up with it.

Being from a large city like St. Louis where vagrants and homeless were arrested or taken to shelters, we wondered how this city could overlook the situation, especially being the well-known country music recording capitol and tourist town in the Midwest.

Later in the afternoon when we stopped at a record store, we mentioned it to a salesman and our concern. He simply explained that the City of Nashville was very tolerant of their homeless people. They were not run off or arrested as one might think.

"After all" he said, "They had come from many areas in the hills around Tennessee and Kentucky with nothing but the clothes on their back and their instruments, to take a chance in this great city to become a famous recording artist or be in the Grand Old Opry"

VAGRANTS OF MUSICLAND

Did you ever drive through Nashville

And see them lying on the lawns

Of the public buildings in the square?

Their life's ambition gone

Their meager clothing tattered

Over bodies frail and thin

With faces gaunt and hollow eyed

clutching half full pints of gin

Who will put them to their rest?

Will an old pine box be made?

That will carry them to a common ground

To be placed in sun or shade?

In search of fame and fortune

They traveled from afar

From Ozark hills and townships

To become great music stars

These poor old souls just stay here

And hover near the scene

Of this country music heartland

Where they once had hopes and dreams

SUNRISE AND SECRETS

By Andrea Doetzel   7-2012
Revised from original published in the
1992-93 winter edition of the
"Cahokian"

Over the vast empty plaza
Silver mist hovers close to the ground
The onset of dawn is unfolding
Distant birds make awakening sounds

Slowly as darkness starts to fade
With the passing of night
The silhouette of a great earthen mound
Emerges in soft amber light

Long shadows are cast on the landscape
A crowning sun bursts into view
Revealing the structures and farmland
Of a culture that flourished and grew

They charted their life by the seasons
Using marker posts set for each one
The planting and harvests continued
Each a festival of the "Great Sun"

The "Sun King" possessed a great power
Chiefs and family among his elite
He demanded a share of the maize crop
Gifts and offerings brought to his feet

Steady growth of a dynamic city
But then came a gradual decline
We have tried to determine the reason
As the mystery remains over time

Today as you glance at the plaza
Silver mist still floats near the ground
As a modern day dawn is unfolding
Distant birds make awakening sounds

Does this mist hold the spirits of old ones
Resting near to guard burial mounds?
Would they have the power to tell us
The secrets of these sacred grounds?

INDIAN SUMMER SUNSET

A September morn, at the Fall Equinox
       Sunrise ceremony today
Word of the festival spread through the land
       Many traveled from far way

Merchants brought gifts and trade goods
       In their long dugout canoes
Chiefs of small nearby hamlets
       Came in search of stories and news

After feasting and new tribal dances
       Elite newborns were honored with names
With the festival evening approaching
       Players cheered at the end of their games

Then thousands converged on the plaza
       Commanded by rhythmic drum sounds
For procession of "Great Sun" their leader
       To the top of his huge earthen mound

Amber glow casts a spell on the city
       In the distance a lone eagle flys
The King traces the sun with his scepter
       As it melts in a violet sky

Now silence observed, only whispers
       Crowds disperse to thatched huts for the night
To build fires and rest weary bodies
       Celebration at next morning light

The soft murmur, a group of priests chanting
       Singing crickets in cornfields nearby
A dog barks at the shadows of campfires
       Far away, a small baby's cry

He surveys his domain from the summit
       Supreme power of this empire he keeps
Sights and sounds of a darkening metropolis
       As mighty Cahokia sleeps

My interpretation of an ancient summer festival at Cahokia Mounds in Collinsville, Illinois.

STORIES

SPIRITS OF THE PLACE

Three visits — April, August & Oct 1990

April 1990 - There is a place that haunts me, it has touched my very soul. The stream flows by and turns there. Over rocks the currents roll. Deep woods surround this haven, the air is always still, tall trees keep it shaded, wild flowers cover the hill. Bluffs in layers line the slope. My new trail cuts around. At the top a place was leveled, nearby lies a strange mound. It would have been a perfect place for ancient ones to stay. Do their ancestors still lie here? Have their spirits gone away? Why does this place draw me? I have a need to know, who wandered in these woodlands a thousand years ago?

August 1990 – The summer air was cool this eve, slight breezes through the trees, as if a voice was whispering. Or was it just the leaves? I took a stroll back through the woods to an eerie place I found. Along the trail I padded, my footsteps made no sound. My canine friend grew restless and he trotted on ahead, but stayed in sight and checked on me, through tall trees I was led. We passed the marshy floodplain, and where the stream turns round, up the curving narrow pathway, to the place of the strange mound. I found the pile of chert chips that intrigued me one Spring day. The dog had started digging there and I discouraged him away. Suddenly he sensed it, letting out peculiar whines. He had discovered something. I feared what I would find. Bending to look closer, I could plainly see that this had been the burial place of a people of mystery.

There was a sudden moaning sound, cold breezes in the air, the kind that chill down to the bone. A voice whispered:

Beware! Let me lie here peacefully, or my spirit will not soar. Disturb thee not this resting place, look upon me no more.

I covered up the old remains, piling rocks upon the grave. No one would dig here ever. This spirit would be saved.

Walking back along the trail and shaking now in fear. Did a Spirit speak to me? What did I really hear?

The eve was close to dusk now as I neared the place called home. I vowed to keep the secret of old bones beneath the stone. Back on my porch I rested, my adventure to an end, and then as leaves swirled in, they spelled out:

 Spirits call you Friend

October 1990 -

The leaves had turned to red and gold, the air was crisp and clear. I wondered now about the "Place" and the strange soul hovering near. Still curious to wander back, but somehow still afraid, to look upon the burial place and the lone stone covered grave. Now and then I heard a voice that seemed to beckon me, to sit upon the sacred ground and hear a spirit's plea. I walked along leaf covered trails and found a place nearby, to sit and think and listen and to watch the clear blue sky. Again I felt the air turn cold, a stillness all around, and then a voice began to speak. It came from near the mound....

I was the leader of my tribe and lived four and thirty years. My last ten were in sorrow and my nights were filled with tears. A young bride I had taken and with child she was that day, as she fetched water from the stream, the earth took her away. On a morning walk down to the spring, the earth made rumbling sounds, great boulders fell down from the slope and crushed her to the ground. She lies beneath the large one, covered all but head and arms.

We could not move the giant stone. Her resting place it formed. Choked with grief and broken, I had to leave her there, and cover up her lovely face and her silky raven hair. We prayed her soul would find its place and I would join with her one day, but I have searched this vast dimension, and she was lost along the way. She seems to live in Your World as if nothing had gone wrong. She haunts these hills and valley, I can hear her childhood song. A strange request I ask of you: Please speak and let her know, about her final resting place and my nearby waiting soul.

I found the giant boulder and leaned against the side. As I spoke to the young girl beneath, large teardrops filled my eyes. "Close by upon the covered mound your soul mate waits for you, for you had lived but died young and his deep love still holds true. He waits now for your spirit, to join with his and soar, to the afterlife beyond this world, where you will live forevermore"

I sensed an apparition floating up beyond the trees, to join with another similar form, and the movement caused a breeze. As I looked up at these two souls, they intertwined and swirled, then quickly disappeared from view as they sped toward their other world.

The autumn air seemed warm again, a peaceful calm all around. No longer that eerie feeling, near the ancient burial mound. At last the spirits freely roamed, but spoke to me again…

When* your *time comes to greet our world, guiding hands we will extend

By Andrea Doetzel 10-15-2012

Condensed from three original poems written about the "Place " on her families Barnhart Property on

April, August and October 1990

THE THREE WEEKS I KNEW BOBBY

By Andrea Doetzel

Bobby Story was his name. He came to our third grade class a few weeks late in the fall semester at Wyman school in South St. Louis back in the early 1950's. They said he was from the country somewhere in Southern Missouri.

We thought everyone young lived in cities by now.

Bobby was introduced to the class and the teacher seated him toward the back in the row by the windows, as that is alphabetically where the R through Z kids sat. The sun streaming in the window made his rusty hair shine. He was clean and well groomed and didn't have a whole face of freckles like most red heads, but was tanned and wore brand new overalls. Later, perhaps self-conscious that these were odd to us, he switched to jeans as I think he wanted to belong.

I had an instant crush on him. Puppy Love at first sight and I caught him looking back at me a lot in class, even though I sat at the front in the first row by the door.

The boys competed for his attention, and they whispered to him in class. He was a novelty I guess. He could tell them things in secret, probably how farm animals copulate and barnyard bull and how he got to drive tractors and stuff.

Other girls ignored him, and acted too goody goody but he did not seem to mind. There was a shy side of him and he was quietly obedient in class. A WEEK WENT BY, Then Monday he was absent. They said he would be back, just broke his wrist jumping off a concrete ash pit next to the alley with a bunch of the boys Friday night. Were these boys daring him, trying to see his country stuff, or was he just being daring and trying to fit in?

When he came back to school he had a brand new cast on his right arm. He was excused from most of the writing in class and some of us were brave enough to ask him if we could write our names on his cast. I signed by his thumb in red ink. I wanted my name to show, not to be hidden by his shirt as he started wearing longer sleeves. I had never done anything that gutsy before and was one of only two girls in class to sign.

ANOTHER WEEK WENT BY and he was absent again. Sick in a hospital they said..... I thought, poor Bobby, how could he be sick? Country kids are healthy and he was a little bigger than the other boys his age. Did we have big bad city germs and give him some?

The THIRD WEEK on Monday, after we all got settled in our desks, the teacher said she had some sad news. Bobby's parents had called her over the weekend and said he died at the hospital. I sat there at my desk looking down for what seemed like an hour. The teacher asked us to take out a piece of paper and as I tried to hide my tears they dripped all over He had been at our school only three weeks and now he was dead and the funeral would be in three days. The class wrote down the name of the funeral parlor on Lafayette Avenue and the times. It was next to the building where my Saturday dancing school was.

That afternoon after school I came home real quiet and my Grandpa noticed. After a while, when I did not want to go in for supper, he asked why and I started crying again and he just pulled it out of me. My Grandpa had heard me talk about the red headed country boy in the weeks before and asked me why I was so interested in him, then teasingly joked that maybe

I was his sweetheart. I blushed…. But now, Grandpa was quietly serious. Grandpa was an employee of Jennings Ramsey of St. Louis where they made funerary goods and caskets. He explained that there would be a place to go called a funeral parlor and that is what the teacher had us write down on the paper. He said people went to the funeral parlor to see the person as a last chance to say goodbye before they went to heaven. He told me I should go. Bobby would just look like he was sleeping, then I could say goodbye in private as the parlor would be sort of like a church.

I did not know what to do as I had never been to a funeral parlor, had just stayed home when great Grandma died a few years back, but then she was 83. We were too young, my sister, brother and 3 cousins, so we read library books at home and were all in school the day she was buried. I kept thinking, how would I go to a funeral parlor to see Bobby Story and what would my mom say? If we weren't allowed to go to Great Grandma's funeral parlor, would she allow me to go to a boys, especially one I liked a lot? Besides, how would I get there? Mom had to attend night school since we moved in with our grandparents because of my mom and dad's divorce.

The next night after supper my Grandpa said to get dressed in my Sunday clothes and we were going to take a bus ride. We got to the funeral parlor and he told me to wait on the steps by the garden area. He walked up and went in the door and seemed at ease shaking hands and talking with a few people who greeted him. I waited by the small pond and watched goldfish swim in the bottom under the sprinkling waterfall. Fall flowers were planted nearby and I thought this was a pretty place even for dead people. It seemed like forever, then Grandpa came out and said we could go in now, but I hesitated as I wanted to sit and watch the fish a little while longer, thinking I really did not know if I wanted to go in this dead people's place. Then Grandpa gently took my hand and we went up the steps as I looked down at the new green carpet.

Every one talked in hushed tones and I only noticed adults in this place, no other children, none of my classmates or teachers at all. A few older ladies smiled at me and then looked away, perhaps sensing my self consciousness. I was led to a room that was empty except for a casket and a few large flower displays. The other people were all across the hall sitting around in chairs. Bobby was lying asleep in a brand new Navy Blue suit. A light shined softly down on him from the ceiling and caught the beauty of his shiny red hair. He looked so peaceful. I stood there looking at him as my grandpa kept his hand on my shoulder. After a few more minutes Grandpa went over and started talking softly to a man in the doorway who was probably the funeral director. Now I think Grandpa may have known him from the funeral business. Quietly I watched Bobby, afraid to breathe and absorbed everything around me and I could smell the sweetness of the flowers as I waited to see if he would move or start breathing too, but nothing happened. I had never seen him in anything but overalls and jeans, but now…. He was in his Sunday best, and so was I….. To say goodbye. They had tried to clean up his cast with some white stuff, probably shoe polish, but my name in red ink by his thumb had bled through, As I looked at his right hand folded over his left I thought….. I had left a mark on Bobby Story and it still showed.

I held back the tears this time but thought it was strange that a person who was so sick and died could look so beautiful. Later my Grandpa said he looked so nice because he was at peace and in care of the angels. It was getting dark and Grandpa put his hand on my shoulder again and said we had to get the next bus home. Politely he shook hands and said goodbye to several of the adults and we walked down the steps to the sidewalk near the bus stop. I talked to no one there that night except Grandpa. I did not even know who Bobby's parents were. I guess that was best, because if I would have talked to anyone they may have asked who I was and I didn't want anyone to complain about my red scribbled name on his cast or know how much I liked Bobby as he may have not been able to have a girlfriend from the city like me.

All the way home I was quiet. Before bed I had a glass of milk and Grandpa sat with me and explained how Bobby died. When he fell from the ash pit and broke his arm, it was a compound fracture with a piece of bone sticking out of his wrist. The hospital where he went thought he had all his shots since he just started school in the city. But he was from the country and maybe they did not need to get shots there. He died of Lockjaw poisoning from the dirt in the wound. Grandpa said I should not be upset because Bobby was in a very beautiful place now, and going back home to the country to be buried near his grandparents.

How sad it was. He did get a germ from the city. In a dirty old ash pit. Even though Grandpa said people who were around barns and stuff were exposed to tetanus toxins. Bobby was probably around that a lot, but it is ironic that his family moved to the city for a better life and then he died. I will never forget Bobby Story and will always be grateful to my Grandpa who helped me understand what death is and took me to say goodbye.

(**<u>This story was written as if I was age eight as I remembered it</u>**)

My Grandmother –A new bride in 1918

Mexico, Mo. 3/19

My Grandmother in my Grandpa's
Army Uniform after being discharged
On March 17, 1919

My Grandfather (right)
And his best friend Frank

Best Friends joking and dressing up
as a married couple with infant

PICNICS IN PEORIA

A hundred years ago 7-15-2012

I found an old moldy smelling photo album in a box of papers and family documents after my mom passed away.   What a jumble of things she had inherited that were left from her parents and many aunts and uncles.   No one wanted to take these things when they cleaned out the house. They were brought to my house and I filled an old cedar chest with death notices, probate papers, divorce settlements, and first communion photos of the 9 siblings of my grandfather. All the relatives had died and my mom was the last one left to care for these ghostly items.

I started looking at all the pictures, picking out my grandparents in several. How dapper my grandfather looked in his suit and hat.   There were some notes on separate slips of paper placed between the pages that my late uncle had written, describing who the people were and where the photos were taken as my grandfather and uncle had looked over the album together in grandfathers last years. My grandfather's handwriting was at the bottom of several photos: Peoria 1912, Redbud IL, 1913, Road to Belleville 1914.

I saw a note on one photo taken when my grandfather met my grandmother at a Picnic in Peoria. There were many pictures of ladies and men enjoying the outdoors with cornfields in the background. The men were dressed up and playing baseball. Some of the ladies were all lying on the grass together in light colored dresses. A grand Picnic at the farm in Peoria August 1912. Baseball in a white shirt and dark slacks? Ladies in long dresses outside in August? Times have changed. This had to be a Sunday event because of the attire.

I was charmed by one where my grandmother was sitting under a grape arbor. Some were funny and they must have enjoyed joking around and dressing up in each other's clothes. There is one with my Grandfathers best friend, and he was making fun of my grandpa being a newlywed. One showed my grandmother a few years later in my Grandpa's army uniform after he came back from the war, in March of 1919.

I was taken away to the past and found out what life was like. My grandparents were young. Then the war and rationing and then Grandpa had to leave. My Grandma and my mom, being a small baby had to move in with relatives in Mexico, MO until the war was over.   So many memories captured with a camera…. No wonder they were cherished. It was the most precious time of their lives and from the worn look of the album, they looked back often. Many years and locations, gathering dust in a bookcase, then stored and forgotten for over 40 years.

What am I to do with these memories? Keep them with this story to pass on to my children and hope they can feel a kinship with these ancestors and the family memories, and compare today's picnics with those of days long ago.

Top left - Grandfather (right) with friends

Top right – Long dresses in August heat

Center left – Sisters below – Grandfather at left top

Center right - Grandfather at bat in Sunday clothes

THE DANCER AND THE NOT SO GENTLE GREEK MAN

By Andrea Doetzel

Saturday night at 10:30 she entered the front door of the Mirage Restaurant and Lounge walking past the long L shaped bar. The bar area was dark and smoky compared to the back dining area where she was headed. The tables were crowded with customers waiting for her performance. Stephano sat in the spotlight on his barstool at the end of the small stage and nodded at her as she went by the band trio. He was playing his Bouzouki and singing the favorite Greek songs this crowd loved.

On her way along the bar, near the front, she noticed a distinguished elderly gentleman, tanned with white hair, wearing one of those old type navy blue fisherman's caps. He was holding a drink and before him sat a standard appetizer plate of Pita bread, tomatoes, feta cheese, and olives.

Sometimes people dined at the bar where they could still see the show, if they were alone, rather than take up room at a table. However most Greeks in the St. Louis area knew each other well, shared tables and socialized by comparing which region or village their families were from. This was especially true of the crowds that frequented this club in the Central West End and at the Athen's Restaurant just down the street.

Entering the dressing room she slid off her caftan, tucked two veils in over her costume and put her finger cymbols in place, listening for the medley Stephano played, as the queue, before her entrance number. As he announced her name over the mike, she danced in, and stepped up on the platform. The spotlight blinded her, but she was in her own zone, the world of her dance, which she had performed many times before. She spun around and swirled the veils, and as the tempo changed, picked up the rhythm with her cymbals as the crowd clapped along into the finale. At the end of her dance they shouted "Opa" and applauded. She was paid by the owner upon leaving the dressing room, and did not stay long afterward to visit with the customers at their tables. She was still new at this club and planned to keep her performances and her social life separate. The band continued playing, but changed to a more lilting melody as it enticed the crowd to get up and folk dance.

Street dressed now, she quietly made her way down the bar toward the front to leave. She approached the elderly gentleman sitting at the end near the door. She could feel his eyes upon her. As she passed, he reached over and grasped her arm, pulling her toward him. He said. "I have never seen you here before, you are new and so different from the rest with your light colored hair. You look nothing like the other dancers." "What is your name again?" She answered, "Elaina".

He said, "Well I am Nikolais, on vacation from Corfu, and I come here every week to listen to the band and see the dancers." Then he reached a hand up to the top of his nose, near the inside, dug a finger in and pulled out a prosthetic eye.

Holding it up to her, he said…. "It was nice to see you dance, Elaina." "I WILL be sure to KEEP AN EYE OUT FOR YOU", Then he spun around on his barstool and reached over with his other hand to try to slap her on the bottom, but she quickly turned and escaped out the door.

1-21-2012

BLACK LIGHTS - VERSUS FLASHLIGHTS

In Barnhart, MO south of Kimmswick, on the east side of Highway 61-67 there used to be an old hardware store called Kohler City Supply. People from miles around came to visit this town and unique store. It was quite a novelty, built out of wooden clapboards with an older dark brown warehouse next door, that had a rickety outside staircase leading up to the second level, where bins of used goods and salvaged parts were displayed. People could get overalls, lawnmower parts, tools and supplies, and if needed, pick up a pair of used false teeth from the barrel next to the old fashioned cash register at checkout. Over the years in the 1950's and 60's a few floods from the nearby Mississippi covered Highway M and 61-67 and the bridge over Glaize Creek, isolating the town. The IGA store, gas station. Ice cream shack and Kohler City Supply, closed for a time but later recovered and again businesses opened in the buildings. Around the late 60's the original dilapidated Kohler City store was leveled. A new concrete block building was constructed in its place lasting many years and selling the same types of goods, except the teeth.

A few decades later the great flood of 93' came and got inside this newer building and after the water went down cleanup began and in a year or so it reopened as a warehouse for an appliance store. The grounds in back of this store next to Glaize creek remained a scruffy brush and log infested floodplain when the owner decided to try and make some money there by putting in a Paintball shooting range. This was directly across the creek and in view of my son's home and my daughter's home further up the ridge. We owned 23 acres of woodlands and home sites but our land was a higher level than the Paintball Park.

Well, the proprietor of the paintball range just piled up old tires and made makeshift huts out of flood damaged pallets and bulldozed in a few hills and foxholes and every summer for 2 years there were kids screaming while the rat tat tat echo of the guns became the norm. This was mostly on weekends and it closed at dark. We tolerated it. The creek was pretty wide and served as a boundary to our property, even though sometimes a boy tried to shoot a pellet at my grandson while he was playing in the yard with the dogs. The venture did not last long and business fell off one summer.

When school started that year the next idea for the store owner's grounds came all of a sudden….. Young men were seen working during the day as a bulldozer came in and shoved the tires and pallets into the creek bank, then cleared a winding trail all through the back of the floodplain. Our road was on top of the bluff that ran along the creek for about a half mile back into a clearing in the woods. This was a dark and spooky place at night. Well, pretty soon there were gates and a ticket booth by the main road in Barnhart. Scary figures hung from trees. Black lights, electrical cords, plus several generators were being installed along this new trail. We watched the progress and then a sign appeared by the highway entrance for a haunted trail. **Admission $7.00 – Opening - October 15 at dark.** The fun started. Speakers with moaning sounds, screaming and hideous wicked laughing reverberated through the valley. Mostly teenagers came in droves to walk the trail after dark to be scared by a ghoul jumping out from behind a bush with a chattering chain saw while someone pulled ropes to swing the bodies of dummies over the creek. Opening week was noisy, and then they added more scary things and more people were hired to shock the crowd.

My son went over to complain about the noise the first week because of the echo and explained we were in a residential area. They brushed off our requests to at least turn down their speakers.

Our other neighbors also complained with no results. My son's job as truck driver got him up at 3:30 A.M. to make his way into the plant to get his truck loaded for his first delivery. He was having trouble getting to sleep at 9:30 P.M. He complained again. Then they piped in rock music which got louder to appeal to more teens as they waited in line before they opened the trail at dark. On weekends the trail stayed open till midnight with constant noise and people screaming.

We all played cards and barbecued on the weekends at my daughter's home and when she let her dog out one Friday night the poor thing took off scared by the noise. She ran along the road overlooking the creek and headed back to the meadow by our family picnic area.

That night at dark we called to our dog as she had not returned. Four of us walked with big flashlights along the bluff road. We could see shadows in the black lights on the trail across the creek as the occasional white sock or T shirt collar glowed, as crowds of scared teens screamed. Continuing we were quite visible to the patrons on the haunted trail. One guy, who was an attendant shouted up to us saying "Who is that up there? What are you doing? "Get out of there! You have no business around here!" Well.... I shouted back: "This is the Property owner up here and your noises scared our dog and she ran back into the woods. We are just looking for her." Then we heard one girl in a crowd of kids shout out. "This sure is a **rip off,** nothing scary here, I want my money back!" Others echoed "Yeah"!

Well our dog came back to us, along the road barking at the noises but at our feet as we tempted her with treats and flashlights led the way back home. When we got to my daughters house we told the rest of the family that our lights and noise distracted the crowds and their trail was not so "Haunted" after all. My son suddenly grinned, then got out his Kawasaki ATV with the big headlights. He took off with a VROOOM, speeding along the bluff road in a cloud of dust while shouting to a new imaginary dog. We continued this same routine each night they were open on weekends.

Word among teens got around fast: Business dropped off sharply on the haunted trail a week before Halloween, and there was nothing they could do about it.

Eeeeeee ha ha ha ha haaaaa…………..

EGGBERT

Most High Schools offer a class that teaches domestic skills to prepare students for adult life in the world they will soon be living. Called Family and Home Planning, Family Living, Family Relations etc.

Full credit is offered for the class. Many teens elect it as an extra if they have free periods or to build up total credits. When my daughter was a sophomore at FOX High School in Arnold, MO she signed up for this class along with a few of her friends and one boy she had just started to date. I will call him "J".

The class content was how to set up a budget, plan meals, pay bills and other domestic chores typical of a new household. Later discussed, the topic of child care and the constant responsibility of it on a 24 hour schedule. Each student was in charge of their own offspring in the form of an EGG child, had to name it, and keep a diary of the schedule it was on. The teacher issued birth certificates for each egg with the name and the day they were first brought to school. If the student wanted to go out on a date or other event or played in sports, they needed to get a responsible person to babysit the egg and log the time spent away from their egg baby. The teachers had used 5 lb sacks of flour at one time for this class but several flour sack babies got spilled in the halls when dropped or thrown creating slipping hazards and cleanup by the janitor.

The night before eggs were due to be introduced into the class, my daughter came home excited about ideas for hers and asked me to help her create something special. We started by hard boiling 3 eggs in case one would crack in the saucepan. Meantime she explained the details needed, like it should reflect its own personality as it would be named. My daughter's distant Cherokee Indian ancestry came to mind and we created a papoose style carrier pouch for her egg out of denim and red bandana scraps from my sewing box. We fixed straps on the pouch so she could wear it around her neck at chest level and still have her hands free while in the halls carrying her purse and books. She colored a cute face on her egg and we made two ponytails hanging down the sides of the face with a long lock of her dark brown hair and tied them off chin length with tiny red ribbon. We were just about finished at 9:00 pm when her new boyfriend "J" called and asked what she was doing. Being in the same class, she asked if he had his egg ready for the next day. He explained "No" he forgot as he had football practice. Then he asked if she would make his egg and bring it the next morning as the domestic class was second hour. She said,"I cannot believe you . Each of us is supposed to make their own egg and name it." You knew about this" Then he begged, said his mother (who was a teacher at the same High School) had a meeting and she couldn't help him as it was getting too late.

We had two extra eggs so reluctantly she said OK. We made a simple baby style egg and since "J" had blonde hair, I cut a small lock of mine and glued it to the top after we colored the egg a light peach to match skin tone with water colors we used on hers. Then she added two light blue eyes and a tiny bow mouth and two dots for the nose. I started calling it Eggbert while we were making it as it turned out SO cute. Then with no pouch to hold it in, I had an idea to make a diaper holder for a stand to prop it up so it would not roll all over once it was set down. I found a white washcloth, cut out a triangle corner and wrapped the egg in it and pinned the front point up with a gold safety pin.

We set it in the diaper and after a special touch from the kitchen it was ready for my daughter to transport safely to "J" before the class the next morning, nestled in it's large paper cup.

Leslea gave "J" the egg we made before advisory and he carried it in the paper cup until second hour, barely looking at it and just relayed a Huh?, then an unimpressed thanks.

Class started and the teacher explained she would now go around the room, look over each egg and write down any special features about it to issue it's Birth Certificate with the chosen name. If anything was to happen to the egg the teacher needed to be notified right away as a Death Certificate had to be issued with an explanation of how it died. If an egg was cracked with the white showing, it was officially dead.

My daughter's Egg made quite an impression on the teacher as she explained her Indian ancestry and the reason for making the Papoose carrier and the features including her ponytails. Each student had their egg child logged into the teacher's notebook with her own observations and when she got around to "J" she thought his Newborn egg was so adorable resting in the diaper. The facial features being so baby like and dainty, she asked if she could pick it up to take a closer look. When lifting it out of the diaper carrier she laughed and said to "J". " Well…. What do we have here?" As she held the diaper up, she tilted it so everyone could see the **RAISIN** we had placed in the bottom the night before. The Class roared with laughter as "J" turned red and shot dagger looks while shaking his fist in my daughter's direction. And the teacher wrote her comments in the notebook about "J's" Egg and the shameful dirty diaper.

Epilogue

Leslea's egg lasted 3 days. A senior running through the school hall toward her reached out his fist and smashed her egg in its papoose. She did not go out with "J" after the second date. He was all hands and she didn't want to wrestle a football player. Little Eggbert? Who knows, probably smashed to oblivion in football practice or left in a locker or desk somewhere to rot.

BACHELOR BLUNDERS

By Andrea Doetzel   1-26-13

My son grew up resourceful and keen in all his ventures. Making the coolest tree house in the woods near our neighborhood, where the local boys hung out all summer. Even on some fall days or an occasional snow day they would build a campfire and roast hot dogs to get away from doing chores at home. On snow days, they would scout the neighborhood first to get a few shoveling jobs for cash, then walk up to the corner Quick shop for candy and snacks to take back in the tree house spending the rest of the day, until they were called home for supper. It was their own private haven, independent for the day, like young bachelors in training

Later, as a 14 yr. old, he had a small business in a basement room where he raised small lab animals and distributed them to chemical testing facilities and pet shops. In high school he was a skate guard in the evenings at the local roller rink. After graduation his first full time job was at a pool maintenance company. Then an opening came up at the beverage company where his father was a driver salesman. He worked his way up in the company and while living at home, saved his money and eventually had enough to make a down payment on 23 acres of property we purchased as a family. We all had plans to live somewhere on the property one day, improving the grounds, keeping the wooded areas as hunting spots, clearing walking trails and a large meadow. Denny wanted to be on his own soon after purchasing the land. At about age 24, he decided to move down, become caretaker and live in a mobile home, as there were already 6 vacant concrete pads set up with plumbing and sewer and electric outlets from an old trailer park the former owners built for construction crews while they built a subdivision up the hill. This was a faster way for a young man to be on his own rather than wait 6 months for builders to construct a frame house. He ordered a new home and worked on the site during his vacations. All things ready, permits and delivery were set up and he moved in and became a bachelor that week.

In the meantime he shopped for housekeeping goods, toaster, microwave, linens, a coffee pot and crock pot. I got a call one night the first week he moved in asking how to make my delicious beef stew in his new crock pot. I told him what to get at the store and suggested a package of Stew Starter which had dried vegetables, and gravy powder. Everything he needed in one carton instead of having to cut up all those vegetables in the morning before work. I explained how to flour and brown the meat, add a few spices and after adding Stew Starter and water, turn the unit on medium to slow cook all day. Dinner would be ready when he got home from work. He was healing from a herniated disk problem in the months before and purchased the mobile home with the circular jetted tub for his back therapy. He was enjoying the comforts of his organized single life.

That evening, after work, he was really looking forward to a hot Jacuzzi bath and a bowl of beef stew.

He ran hot water in the tub, and added a few squirts of dishwashing liquid to use for bubble bath. Turned on the tub jets and went to the kitchen to check the crock pot and set out a bowl for supper.

A few minutes later in the bathroom he saw a huge growing igloo shaped mound of bubbles climbing toward the ceiling while he had been in the kitchen. It took a while to clean up the foam as he swatted at it with towels. This made huge clusters of bubbles that floated around the room.

 After using several towels to clean up, he now had an extra load of laundry to contend with and the water left in the tub was cold, so he headed to the kitchen with the towels to drop in the washer and planned to eat first and worry about a bath later. Spooning up the stew, he noticed it did not smell or taste quite like mine. The beef stew meat had a strange gray cast and looked slimy and the gravy had an odd taste. Even his Chocolate Lab sniffed it and turned away.

 I got a call later that night and he told me about the tub, I told him a few DROPS, not squirts of dish washing liquid would have been enough for his bath. Then I asked about the stew, found out he had not browned and floured the stew meat in the morning as he did not want to dirty a pan, so just dumped it in the crock pot and added the carton of Stew Starter, water and a few spoons of cinnamon, the only available "spice" he had on hand.   No bath, no supper fit for a man, or even the dog, and a quiet evening at home eating cereal and milk.

Epilogue

My son, now an excellent cook and barbecue chef has come a long way.

EXPLORING WESTERN GHOST TOWNS

Every few years, I used to get restless to go out west on my summer vacations. I loved to wander up along the mountain jeep trails and visit the ghost towns that were abandoned years before when the local gold or silver mines were played out. The miners and families left and ventured to the newer areas in hopes of a strike close to another town where they could be close to a supply store or boarding house for lodging until they could build their own cabin after striking it rich. Isolation was the main peril as when a major snowstorm or illness struck the area, or in spring when snow melt washed out the dirt roads and closed the major passes, they were left on their own to survive.

If the veins of precious metals were abundant, the nearby settlements grew as miners moved into the back hills on simple lots staked out for homes. In the main areas of town other buildings emerged, a small one room school house, a local church and town hall. These towns were given unique names by the founders such as:

Tin Cup, Pitkin, Alma, St. Elmo, Cripple Creek, Victor, Central City, Creede. Wherever there was progress in a town, whether large or small, eventually, and to the challenge of the wives, the popular local saloon was built and thrived. Sometimes the first pub was started in the back corner of the local store.

Some of the miners who had not established a claim of their own, worked long days for the local mine on the outskirts of town. When they were paid late on Friday night they stopped at the pub to cash in their voucher and have a few drinks or food that was offered there before walking the long trail to their cabin, with wife and children waiting and supper held on the stove. Many miners arrived home late and penniless as they drank and gambled away their entire weeks' salary. A mother would sometimes send a young son over after dark to beg the father to come home for supper instead of eating at the saloon.

When you venture through these back roads, some trails just end in a patch of waist high prairie grass. Some railroad tracks stop as they lead into a mountainside that was too vast to blast through and were never used for anything except a track for ore carts to transport rock hacked off of the surface by locals in search of a new strike. On the road to some towns you can drive through tunnels cut through a mountain and wind up in an abandoned area where you must turn back around. Often you see a pile of stones just heaped up along a trail with a metal cross at one end. The grave of one who passed in the harsh winter in the mountains and had to be put to rest in haste when travel to town was impossible.

When you see a ghost town below from the crest of the highest ridge and look over the area in silence you can take yourself back in time. As you look at the gaunt weathered skeletons of the structures it is humbling to guess at their identity by the features.

The little church with only a tilted steeple sticking out amidst collapsed walls. The old school house with peeling white paint still visible on one side. A heap of gray curled clapboards atop half a crumbling foundation wall. Higher up in the mountain near the main mine building and built into the side of the hill, an old two seater outhouse tilts on its side, the doors blown off with weathered hinges still nailed to the frame. Old abandoned mines shafts dot the hillsides and are boarded up with criss crossed timbers and warning signs to block the entrance by the National Forestry. Further down the ridge near the main area of the town, rusty smoke stacks peek out of a row of crumbled heaps of unsalvaged lumber. Probably a streets main row of small homes. A peek inside a broken window of an old cabin shows yellowed newspaper peeling from the inside walls. Old crates and a dented tea kettle under a pile of rain soaked debris. Rusty mattress springs among a box of old moldy high top shoes. Almost as if the home had been abandoned in haste.

You can almost imagine the sights and sounds of a day long ago. Children's laughter and songs as they played in the school yard. The voices of the women as they visited with each other while walking along the trail to the boardwalk in town for the days shopping. A distant train whistle that echoes up the ridge from the next village. The clink clink of pick axes from the closest shaft mixed with the booming sound of a charge set off further away. The tracks clattering as a cart of broken rocks comes rolling down to the chat pile at the bottom of the hill. Smoke from a fireplace chimney floats up in the cool mountain atmosphere and the smell of cooking still lingers in the air.

Some of the larger towns survived over the years and with some mining, have mostly become major tourist attractions. Old Opera Houses and Banks, Saloons and Gambling Halls, Restaurants next to rows and rows of gift shops. Train rides are offered through tunnels into scenic mountain passes and returning after following a loop back to the main station. A graveyard atop a hill with the markers and headstones of some of the famous outlaws or townspeople with local legends and lore. A story of a broken hearted miner who painted the face of his sweetheart on the bar room floor and then fell over the image as he shot himself.

I have seen many ghost towns on my trips, but I prefer to venture to the smaller isolated towns and areas. That is where you can still reflect on the history of the lives of the settlers and enjoy the vast unspoiled beauty as it was in days long ago.

My 13 year old daughter however, grew weary of the back country solitude and had an urge for more action in a bigger town after 4 days of exploring the places I picked. We had thought the educational aspect of learning about the life of past generations in mining towns and to see where they lived would be good subject matter for her to write her essay when she went to school in the fall, when teachers asked about summer vacations. So promises were made to go to the closest big boom town on the way back before heading home in a few days. Another stop in a remote area proved to be more adventurous for her when we found a recently abandoned Ghost town a little northwest of Salida, Colorado. The town had about 6 deserted homes and many warning signs that the water was contaminated. Curious, we walked to the creek and town pump area to discover the carcass of a huge bloated black and white cow, lying near the water's edge that had recently wandered in from the back woods and drank the water.

A few graves with stone mounds over them, that were surrounded by iron fencing made us question if these were from someone who died from poisoned water, but the iron fencing was ornate and appeared much older than the houses that had 50's construction features. We did not see a mine shaft anywhere near the homes. After walking around to the edge of town, my daughter then discovered shiny debris chips on the ground near the last house and went on to discover these particles had flaked off the face of a short bluff nearby. There had been evidence of others picking away at the face of the rock so she went up and started chipping away to get her share of this magic "gold" that turned out to be Mica layers. Later when we walked into one of the old houses, we discovered a pink paper border with black naked lady silhouettes pasted along the ceiling of a small bathroom.. Giggling the rest of the day we stopped for supper in the nearest town and then headed back to the main route to find an RV park for the night. Plans for the next day were to head to Cripple Creek in the morning for the adventures my daughter craved, with 2 weeks allowance burning a hole in her pocket.

Some say the town of Cripple Creek got its name from the many rough stones that were sunk in the creek bed and the damage it caused to the legs of livestock crossing over. This town was in a remote area but was still populated because one of the mines was still active. Main Street through town had tall 3 story brick buildings that used to be hotels, dance halls, boarding houses and saloons for the large population of 35,000 at the turn of the century. The present town still had shows in the old Opera House and dozens of new shops, restaurants and antique stores with apartments on the upper levels. We found a lot of gift shops that had everything a teen would want. Candy, junk jewelry, games, party favors, funny postcards, lip gloss, hats and plenty of girlie stuff.

There was a famous street on a lower level in back of Main Street that overlooked the actual creek area. There we saw these cute little one room shacks all in a row. This was the towns "Red Light" district and these "cribs" as they called them were for the ladies of the night. The lady would have her name in the window next to a red light and invite gents in for the evening. If the light was out, the occupants were busy. My daughter was sort of surprised by this so I got a pamphlet about it to read later rather than take the popular tour through one crib and answer her questions. So, quickly back to Main Street to shop at one of the gift boutiques in a large hotel. There we found unusual things such as a basket of old brass coins or tokens, big as half dollars, for sale near the cash register for 25 cents each. There was some sort of tarnish on them over the writing and some had names of different hotels, but they looked old and charming. We bought several for souvenirs and put them in the bag with our post cards, bandanas and dream catchers. After eating Buffalo burgers and my discovery in another shop of a small perfectly round tumbleweed to take back, we headed toward the main highway before evening.

On to Colorado Springs the next morning through scenic Gold Camp Road and then we headed east toward home with many happy memories of the past week . At rest stops we looked over our treasures and I read about the cute shacks and the hotels in the Red Light district. The Madame of Cripple Creek operating from a major hotel was respected by everyone, so much so, that the entire town closed down for her funeral procession when she finally died. The crib section was organized by class, such as younger girls and women at one end and older women and those of lesser quality were further up the row. Halfway home and dividing up the rock candy and the interesting brass tokens with my daughter I happened to read a few, in a better light than the gift shop counter of the Hotel. These were tokens purchased by patrons of several of the old named establishments in town. I THEN became the owner of all these coins… Each coin had similar wording such as: **"Good for ALL NIGHT"** and on the flip side, **"Free Bath Included."**

By Andrea Doetzel 7-2013

PIONEER JOURNEY

In spring they left Missouri, heading to the West
      Their wagons rolled toward Oregon, a new life, their quest

Dreams of fertile Promised Land, leaving families in the east
      Perhaps the dream, more for the men, for some women, the least

Many hardships were expected, a list of things made clear
      Along this 6 month journey, there would be many tears

Some could not part with certain things, that held memories of their past
      But hid these sacred treasures in the bottom of their packs.

A rocking chair piled high with goods, stored in the wagon back
      To use when a new child was born, if timing was on track

Sometimes on a rugged hill, or halfway through a river crossing
      Wagon masters could lighten loads, and saw to, the tossing

A new life would start with nothing, just log cabins and bare floors
      Furniture built of crates for now, later pack trains could bring more

The challenge of quite simple chores, at times a hardship or a pain
      Cooking meals on open fires, under wagons in the rain

Often along the dusty trail, lonely graves came into view
      Cholera had run its course and did not spare these few
Many more reminders left on the road by those ahead
      Pony tracks and Indian spears caused uncertainty and dread

A doll dropped or discarded, a broken barrel, still quite new
      Bones of a worn out pack horse, a mud caked baby shoe

Some continued on with heartache, often a wife without her man
      The strong one lost along the way, no hope now for his plan

But as they reached their destination, most had ambitions realized
      Homesteads and new cabins, beneath spacious western skies

Andrea Doetzel 5-2013

STOP, LOOK AND LISTEN

Time to Stop, Look and Listen

As we awaken every day

Many wonders go unnoticed

As we go on our busy way

Step outside your front door

and just listen as birds sing

Their songs are meant to calm us

As we start our chores and things

Take your morning cup of coffee

Sit a moment if you can

Relax in Nature's beauty

Which was meant for every man

Time will pass to evening

The day filled with each event

But remember peaceful mornings

And all the gifts that God has sent

By Andrea Doetzel 7-17-2012

For **Burnell Petry,**

The Sugar Creek Wanderer.

Who has given us this good advice

Your Special Garden

Bloom where you are planted
Is what you always seem to do

Each challenge or endeavor
You always follow through

And all along life's pathway
Wherever seeds are sown

You'll have the thrill of looking back
To see how much you've grown

ANGEL AWARENESS

There is a Special Angel
Who has a broken wing
She cannot fly among the clouds
Where Herald Angels sing

She can only soar in circles
With wounded wing tucked down
Her mission is to seek dark clouds
And slowly glide around

Sometimes a gray cloud follows us
And fills our life with dread
As we deal with family crisis
And uncertainty ahead

This is the Angel's purpose
While hovering above
To gently calm and guide us
And remind us of God's love

CHUBBY CHERUBS

Why are most cherubs naked

As depicted in old art?

Cutely posing with fat hands

Folded across the heart

Their wings are all too tiny

Heads full of golden curls

You may see the difference

Between the boys and girls

Do they grow up to be Angels

With special tasks compiled?

Or gently frolic in the clouds

Forever as a child

I think they have a purpose

When they cross the heavenly path

As they try to fly up off the clouds

They make the Angels laugh

Morning Prayer

Oh Lord, as I wake up today

Give me strength and guide my way

Help me through my fears within

And turn me from the path of sin

Shelter me beneath your arms

And keep me safe away from harm

I am happy in your guiding Love

And rejoice when I look up above

To see the sun and clouds and sky

Where you watch over from on high

Amen

Printed in the United States
By Bookmasters